Usborne STEM

SCIENCE

Scribble Book

THE DISCOVERIES IN THIS BOOK WERE SCRIBBLED BY:

Written by
ALICE JAMES

Illustrated by
PETRA BAAN

Designed by
Emily Barden

Series editor **Rosie Dickins**

Series designer **Zoe Wray**

Additional content by **Darran Stobbart**

Expert advice from
CAROLE KENRICK
Science teacher and
education consultant

CONTENTS

What is science? _ 4

Think like a scientist _ _ _ _ _ _ _ _ _ _ _ _ _ _ _ _ _ 6

All about you _ 8

Planet explorer _ _ _ _ _ _ _ _ _ _ _ _ _ _ _ _ _ _ _ 12

Rainbow refractor _ _ _ _ _ _ _ _ _ _ _ _ _ _ _ _ _ 14

Paper science _ _ _ _ _ _ _ _ _ _ _ _ _ _ _ _ _ _ _ 16

Animal identifier _ _ _ _ _ _ _ _ _ _ _ _ _ _ _ _ _ 20

Making a move _ _ _ _ _ _ _ _ _ _ _ _ _ _ _ _ _ _ _ 22

Light maze _ 26

Snowflake science _ _ _ _ _ _ _ _ _ _ _ _ _ _ _ _ _ 27

The sky at night _ _ _ _ _ _ _ _ _ _ _ _ _ _ _ _ _ _ 28

Perfectly adapted _ _ _ _ _ _ _ _ _ _ _ _ _ _ _ _ _ 30

Moving pictures _ _ _ _ _ _ _ _ _ _ _ _ _ _ _ _ _ _ 32

Where in the world _ _ _ _ _ _ _ _ _ _ _ _ _ _ _ _ 35

Mirror writing _ _ _ _ _ _ _ _ _ _ _ _ _ _ _ _ _ _ _ 36

Feel the force _ _ _ _ _ _ _ _ _ _ _ _ _ _ _ _ _ _ _ 38

Power to the people _ _ _ _ _ _ _ _ _ _ _ _ _ _ _ 40

Search for stars, planets and meteors in the night sky.

Camouflage a snake to hide it in its rainforest home.

Turning turbines ---------------------- 42

Through the microscope ---------------- 43

Seeing light -------------------------- 44

Hot and cold -------------------------- 46

Animal journeys ----------------------- 48

Skeletons ----------------------------- 50

Butterfly or moth? -------------------- 53

Robot designer ------------------------ 54

Tricking your eyes -------------------- 56

The Periodic Table -------------------- 58

Nanotechnology ------------------------ 60

Infection ----------------------------- 64

The solar system ---------------------- 66

Fingerprints -------------------------- 71

Thought experiments ------------------- 72

Breakthrough! ------------------------- 74

Answers ------------------------------- 76

Acknowledgements ---------------------- 80

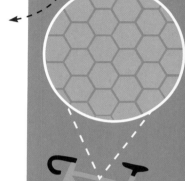

Map the migrations of animals across the world.

Design a vehicle using super-strong nanotubes.

Uncover the discoveries of famous scientists.

WHAT IS SCIENCE?

Science is all about INVESTIGATING, EXPERIMENTING and EXPLORING, to find out how things work – from planets in outer space to tiny particles inside atoms.

Scientists ask questions like:

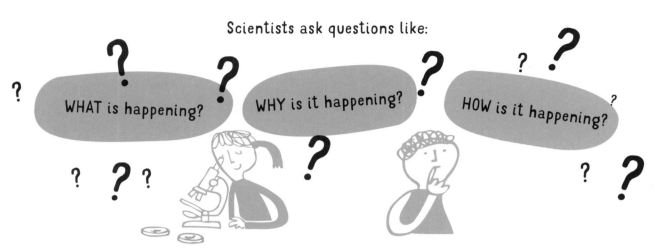

WHAT is happening?

WHY is it happening?

HOW is it happening?

There are three main branches of science.

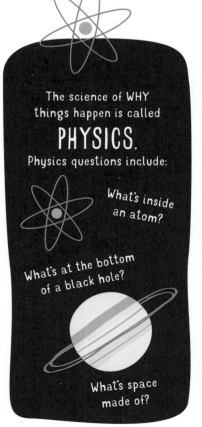

The science of WHY things happen is called **PHYSICS.**

Physics questions include:

What's inside an atom?

What's at the bottom of a black hole?

What's space made of?

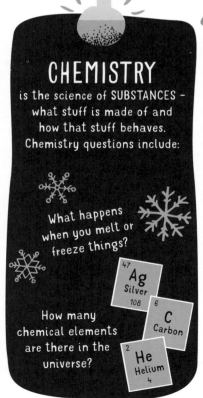

CHEMISTRY is the science of SUBSTANCES – what stuff is made of and how that stuff behaves. Chemistry questions include:

What happens when you melt or freeze things?

How many chemical elements are there in the universe?

47
Ag
Silver
108

6
C
Carbon

2
He
Helium
4

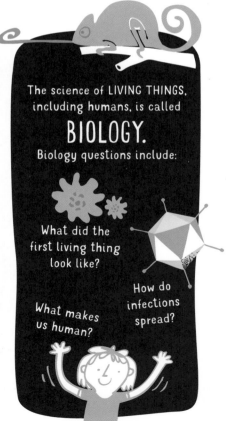

The science of LIVING THINGS, including humans, is called **BIOLOGY.**

Biology questions include:

What did the first living thing look like?

How do infections spread?

What makes us human?

WHAT'S IN THIS BOOK?

You don't need a laboratory full of equipment to do science. It's all about asking questions, and trying to find answers. This book is full of things to...

DESIGN

EXPLORE

Imagine

INVENT

SOL VE

TEST

WHAT WILL YOU NEED?

For most of the book, you'll only need this book and a pencil. For some you might also need paper, glue or clear tape and scissors.

USBORNE QUICKLINKS

To download copies of the templates in this book, and for links to websites with more science experiments, go to **www.usborne.com/quicklinks** and type in the keywords: 'scribble science'. Please follow the online safety guidelines at the Usborne Quicklinks website.

THINK LIKE A SCIENTIST

Scientists usually start by asking a QUESTION about the world around them.

Use this space to jot down any scientific questions you can think of about how or why something happens.

WHAT?

HOW?

WHY?

Why do people have memories?

Do penguins sneeze?

Are there aliens?

What is time?

Do heavy things fall faster than light things?

After asking a question, scientists design an EXPERIMENT to TEST their ideas. Pick one of your questions, and scribble down ways you could test it, using the ideas on the right as inspiration.

QUESTION:

WAYS TO TEST IT:

Scientists call this the METHOD.

Then, if you can, try testing your question. Write down any notes and results here.

RESULTS:

CONCLUSION:

Do your results tell you anything?

ARE THERE ALIENS?

Go to every planet and see what lives there.

Beam signals into space and see if anything responds.

DO HEAVY THINGS FALL FASTER THAN LIGHT THINGS?

Drop heavy and light objects from the same height and see which lands first.

Feather and rock dropped from a chair - landed at same time.

Book and paper clip dropped from a table - landed at same time.

For experiments to PROVE anything, they need to be done multiple times and get the SAME results again and again.

If you CAN'T test your question yourself, (e.g. search for aliens...) look it up online or in a book to see what other people think.

Some questions can't be tested at all, so scientists do "thought experiments." Go to pages 72-73 for more.

ALL ABOUT YOU

NAME: _ _ _ _ _ _ _ _ _ _ _ _ _ _ _ _ _ _   DATE OF BIRTH: _ _ _ _ _ _ _ _ _ _ _ _ _ _

HAIR COLOR

Circle or tick the color of your hair.

HAIR TYPE:

☐ Straight

☐ Wavy

☐ Curly

Add a color here if yours isn't shown.

Your hair color is decided by chemical instructions called GENES in your body cells. Red hair is caused by a rare form of a gene called MC1R, that just 1% of people have.

EYE COLOR

Circle or tick all the colors in your eyes. Use a mirror to double check, if you're not sure.

Color this eye to look like your own.

The colored part is called the IRIS. The color comes from a pigment called MELANIN. The more melanin you have, the darker your iris appears.

A dark ring around the iris is called a LIMBAL RING.

Do you have a limbal ring?

☐ Yes

☐ No

LEFT- OR RIGHT-HANDED

☐ Left   ☐ Right

Scribble quickly
in this box.

LEFT-HANDED
people usually
scribble this way.

RIGHT-HANDED
people usually
scribble this way.

Try writing your name with the hand you DON'T normally use.
Most people find this very tricky.

If you can do it easily,
you are one of the
rare people who are
AMBIDEXTROUS – able to
use either hand.

- -

DOMINANT EYE

☐ Left   ☐ Right

To see things, your brain combines images from both eyes, but
most people have a DOMINANT EYE – one their brain favors.
Try this simple experiment to find your dominant eye.

Make a triangle with
your hands. Frame
an object in the gap,
like this.

Close each eye in turn.
If the object JUMPS or
MOVES when you close
one eye, THAT eye
is dominant.

Almost two
thirds of people
are right-eye
dominant.

LIGHTNING REACTIONS

Test your REFLEXES using the ruler on the cover of this book.

------ Find the ruler on the left side of the back cover.

1. Hold the book in your right hand, with the ruler facing you. Make sure 0 is at the bottom.

2. Let go, and try to catch the book in your left hand as fast as you can.

3. Look at the ruler. The number closest to your thumb is your score.

Have a few tries to see if you can improve.

Score 1: _ _ _ _ _ _ _ _ _ _ _ _ _ _ _ _ _ _

Score 2: _ _ _ _ _ _ _ _ _ _ _ _ _ _ _ _ _ _

Score 3: _ _ _ _ _ _ _ _ _ _ _ _ _ _ _ _ _ _

A LOWER NUMBER
= A FASTER REFLEX

It's even better if a friend drops the book for you, as you really have to REACT. Try going against each other, and see who is fastest.

Person 1	Person 2

PUMPING HEART

Place your hand flat on your chest and feel your heart beating.

85, 86, 87

Count how many beats you feel in one minute. That's your HEART RATE.

01:00

RESTING HEART RATE _ _ _ _ _ _ _ _ _ _ beats per minute

AGE	AVERAGE BEATS PER MINUTE
5-6	75-115
7-9	70-110
10 and older	60-100

Young people usually have faster heart beats than older people.

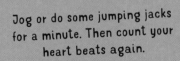

Jog or do some jumping jacks for a minute. Then count your heart beats again.

HEART RATE AFTER EXERCISE

_ _ _ _ _ _ _ _ _ _ beats per minute

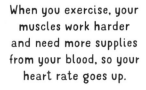

When you exercise, your muscles work harder and need more supplies from your blood, so your heart rate goes up.

PLANET EXPLORER

Scientists use robotic vehicles known as ROVERS like the one below to investigate and explore the surface of Mars, the Moon and asteroids. They search for traces of chemicals, water and signs of life.

Camera to take photographs of the planet

Radio transmitter to send information back to Earth

Solar panels for power

Laser that can investigate rocks and soil

Chunky wheels to get over the tough terrain

NAME: Opportunity Rover

PLANET: Mars

MISSION: Investigating rocks and craters, in particular to look for traces of water.

Design your own rover to
explore another planet here.

THINK ABOUT...

Which planet is it going to?

What is the rover looking for?

Where does its power come from?
Batteries? Sunlight?
A radioactive power pack?

How does it
send messages
back to Earth?

BEEP BEEP

How does it move?
Wheels? Tracks?
Hopping legs?

How will it get
over rocks, or
through soft sand?

NAME: _

PLANET: _

MISSION: _

_ _

RAINBOW REFRACTOR

Ordinary light looks white, but it's actually a mix of colors.
Light travels in waves of different lengths, and each wavelength has its own color.
You can split them apart using a chunk of glass known as a PRISM.

When light hits a prism, it is split apart into the SPECTRUM, revealing seven visible colors of light.

As light passes through the prism, the waves of light BEND. This process is known as REFRACTION.

Red
Orange
Yellow
Green
Blue
Indigo
Violet

White light

Continue the bands of colored light to the middle of the page.

A RAINBOW forms when sunlight shines through raindrops. The raindrops act like tiny prisms, splitting the light into the spectrum.

RED light travels in LONG waves, and
VIOLET light travels in SHORT waves.

Long waves of light
are stretched out.

The high part is
called a crest.

Waves with few crests
in a given stretch are
called LOW FREQUENCY.

This distance
is known as a
WAVELENGTH.

Short waves of light
are bunched up.

Waves with lots of
crests in a given
stretch are called
HIGH FREQUENCY.

⊢— Wavelength —⊣

Join the dots below to make
waves of each color.

PAPER SCIENCE

FOLD

Take a standard piece of paper, and fold it in half as many times as you can, until it gets too thick to fold any more.

How many folds did you manage?

WALK-THROUGH

Copy the template on the right, or download it from the Usborne QUICKLINKS website.

Cut along ALL the white lines. Fold the page in half lengthways to cut the lines coming from the middle.

Cut down the middle too, between the two points marked.

Open it up as wide as it will go.

Put it over your head, and try to fit your body through it.

Did you fit through?

SCRUNCH

Take two identical pieces of paper and scrunch them up.

Unscrunch them, and draw along some of the main fold lines you've made.

Compare the patterns you create. What do you notice? Do they look different?

You can try it with more pieces of paper too. You'll probably find they all look different.

Turn the page to see the science behind all these experiments.

Cut all white lines

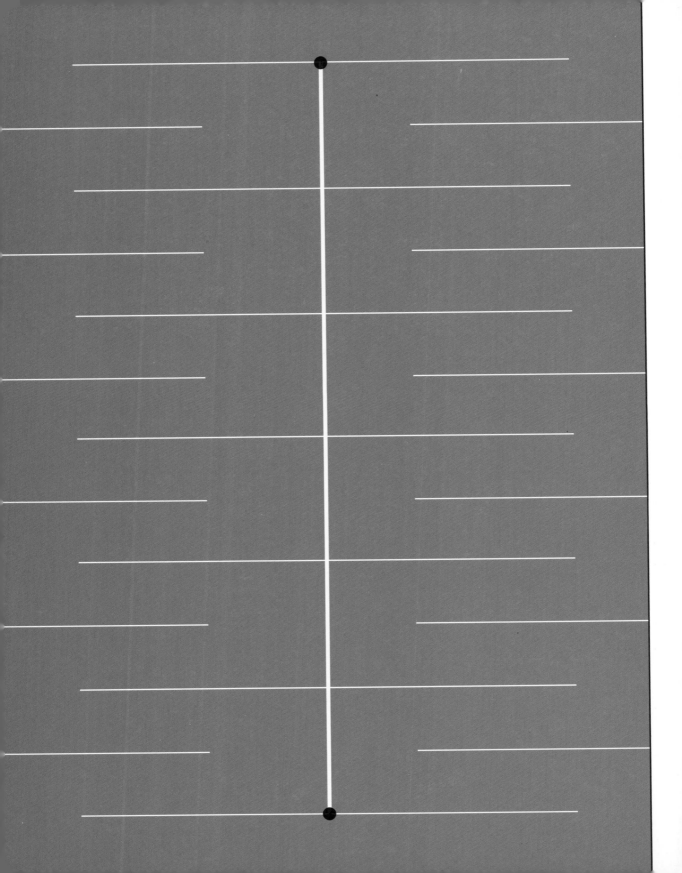

RESULTS

FOLD

Ordinary paper can only be folded SIX or SEVEN times before it's too thick. Everytime the page is folded in half, its THICKNESS DOUBLES. Doubling makes things really big, really fast, in a process known as EXPONENTIAL GROWTH.

If you could fold the paper in half 103 times, it would be thicker than the width of the universe.

WALK-THROUGH

By adding the cuts, you increase the PERIMETER of the piece of paper – the distance all the way around its edges.

You will probably find the new perimeter is big enough that you can fit through the hole in the middle.

SCRUNCH

Paper crumples in a very UNPREDICTABLE way. Scientists think that no two crumpled pieces of paper will EVER have exactly the same folds.

Scrunched paper is also extremely strong.

TEST IT:
Take a scrunched ball of paper and try to crush it flat. Try putting books on top of it, or even standing on it. You'll probably find you can't make it completely flat.

ANIMAL IDENTIFIER

Biologists put animals into broad groups, depending on the type of body they have. Each of these big groups is known as a PHYLUM. They help biologists work out how species are related to each other. Dividing species up into groups is called CLASSIFICATION.

Think of any animal. Draw or write it here, then follow the key to classify it.

Follow the chart to classify these animals. Write them into the white panels below.

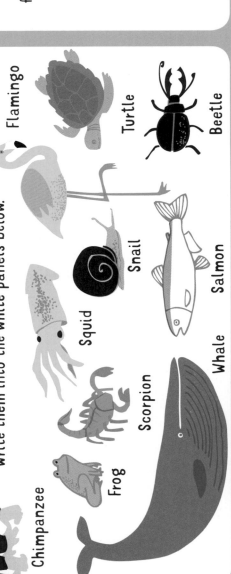

Chimpanzee
Frog
Scorpion
Whale
Squid
Snail
Salmon
Flamingo
Turtle
Beetle

START

Does it have a hard skeleton INSIDE?

YES — Animals WITH an internal skeleton and a hard backbone are called VERTEBRATES.

NO — Animals WITHOUT an internal skeleton are called INVERTEBRATES.

Is it hard on the OUTSIDE?

NO

YES

Is its body split into clear SECTIONS? Can you see a separate head, body and legs?

NO

YES

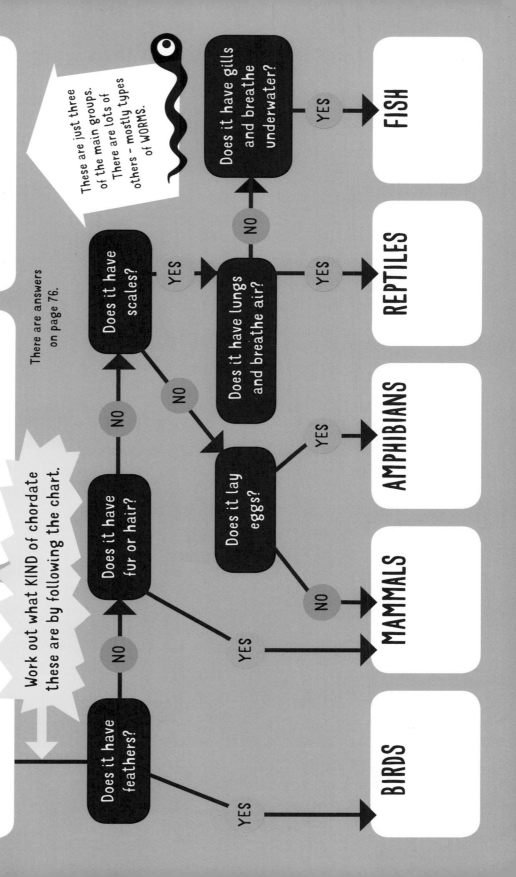

PHYLUM: CHORDATES

Most big animals fall into this category.

PHYLUM: MOLLUSKS

Mollusks are generally soft-bodied. But some, like snails and clams live in hard shells.

PHYLUM: ARTHROPODS

Arthropods have a hard external skeleton called an EXOSKELETON. Their bodies are split into sections, called SEGMENTS.

These are just three of the main groups. There are lots of others – mostly types of WORMS.

There are answers on page 76.

Work out what KIND of chordate these are by following the chart.

Does it have feathers?
YES → **BIRDS**

NO

Does it have fur or hair?
YES → **MAMMALS**

NO

Does it have scales?
YES → **Does it have lungs and breathe air?**
YES → **REPTILES**
NO → **Does it have gills and breathe underwater?**
YES → **FISH**

NO → **Does it lay eggs?**
YES → **AMPHIBIANS**
NO → **MAMMALS**

Making a move

A robot can't do anything without a set of instructions, known as a PROGRAM, which tells it EXACTLY what to do.

This robot can follow three basic instructions.

Instructions

Go forward　　　Quarter turn counter-clockwise　　　Quarter turn clockwise

This program will get it through the maze.

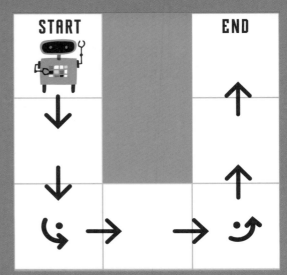

Program A

Continue Program B to get the robot through to the end.

Program B

Program C

Program C is created from Programs A and B, and will get the robot through the large maze. Add in the missing steps.

MEEP

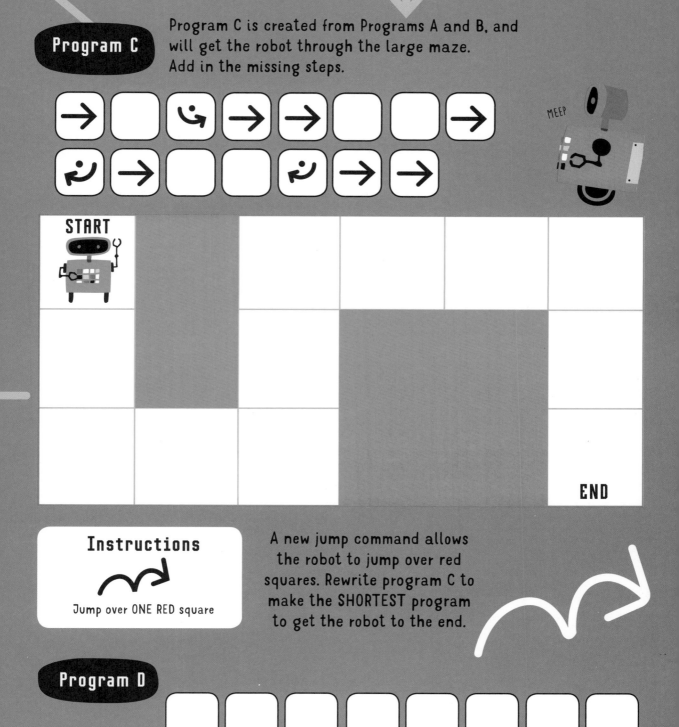

Instructions

Jump over ONE RED square

A new jump command allows the robot to jump over red squares. Rewrite program C to make the SHORTEST program to get the robot to the end.

Program D

Sometimes a robot doesn't do what is expected – usually because there are errors in the program, known as "bugs." Fixing them is known as DEBUGGING.

The robot above is trying to get through a maze – but its program isn't working.

Broken Program

Look through the program and circle the instructions that are WRONG.

Debugged Program

Now write a debugged, correct program.

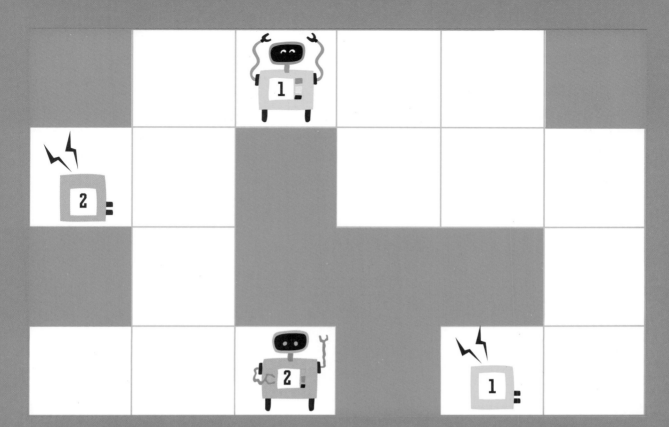

Each of these robots need to get to its matching charging point. Below are the programs to get them there. Which program is for which robot? Write the number on the lines.

MEEP

Program E Robot: _ _ _ _ _ _ _ _

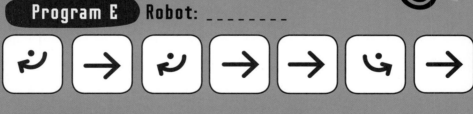

Program F Robot: _ _ _ _ _ _ _ _ _ _ _ _ _

Find answers to all of these on pages 76-77.

Light maze

The waves that make up light always travel in a STRAIGHT LINE,
changing direction when they hit something solid.
When light bounces off a mirror, it creates a REFLECTION.

Light bounces off a mirror at
exactly the same angle it hits at.
So light hitting at 45°
is reflected at 45° too,
making a RIGHT ANGLE.

45°
45°
90°
Right angle

Continue the path
the light would take.
Which letter will
it light up?

BLEEP
BLOOP

Mirror

Light ----

A   B   C   D   E   F   G   H

Go to page 77 for the answer.

SNOWFLAKE SCIENCE

Snowflakes are ICE CRYSTALS that form around specks of dust in the sky.
A snowflake's shape changes as it falls, making each one UNIQUE.
Fill in the arms of these snowflakes, so each snowflake is different.

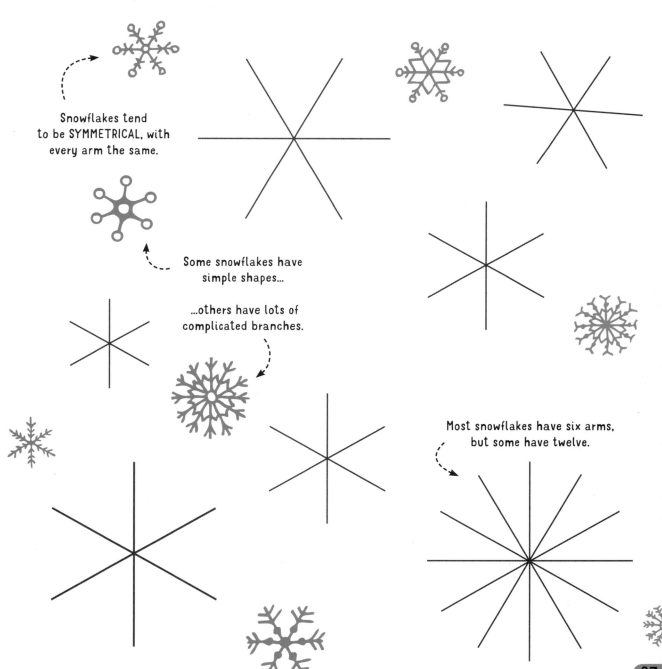

Snowflakes tend
to be SYMMETRICAL, with
every arm the same.

Some snowflakes have
simple shapes...

...others have lots of
complicated branches.

Most snowflakes have six arms,
but some have twelve.

THE SKY AT NIGHT

ASTRONOMERS and ASTROPHYSICISTS study the night sky to learn about the universe. Here are some of the things they look out for...

STARS can be identified by their trademark twinkle, which happens when their light is bent and disrupted by Earth's atmosphere.

PLANETS DON'T twinkle. They're much closer to Earth, and light bouncing off them doesn't bend as much.

VENUS is the closest planet to Earth, and so is the brightest. Venus is easiest to spot at sunrise and sunset.

MARS has a faint reddish glow, because the surface is covered in rusty iron.

METEORS are pieces of space rock falling through Earth's atmosphere, producing a bright streak.

WHOOSH

Sometimes called "shooting stars"

SATELLITES are human-made objects orbiting Earth really fast.

The largest and easiest satellite to spot is the INTERNATIONAL SPACE STATION. It looks like a moving white dot, that doesn't flash like planes do.

THE MOON
From Earth, the Moon is the brightest and most recognizable feature of the night sky.

The Moon doesn't produce its own light – it reflects light from the Sun.

Look at this view of the night sky, as seen through a telescope.
Using the information opposite, what can you identify?

HOW MANY CAN YOU SPOT?

Stars _____

Planets _ _ _ _

Meteors _ _ _ _ _

Satellites _ _ _ _

Moons _ _ _ _ _

The answers are on page 77.

Astronomers group the stars together in familiar shapes known as CONSTELLATIONS – like this one, URSA MAJOR, or The Bear.

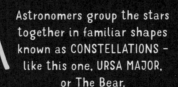

Above Ursa Major is POLARIS, the North Star, which can be used to find North.

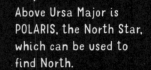

Sailors used to use constellations to help them find their way.

The seven brightest stars in Ursa Major are easiest to spot, and are known as THE BIG DIPPER.

Can you spot Ursa Major above?

PERFECTLY ADAPTED

Plants and animals change over time to suit and thrive in the enviroment where they live. Scientists call this process ADAPTATION.

Here are some common adaptations:

Great EYESIGHT for life in the dark

SPEED to outrun prey

Fancy PATTERNS and COLORS to attract partners

Can you think of an animal for each of the adaptations below? Draw or write them in the boxes.

Sharp TEETH to hunt

ANTLERS or HORNS to fight

FUR to keep WARM

CAMOUFLAGE to hide

Rainforests are full of plants and animals that are well adapted to the crowded, leafy environment.

Trees in the rainforest have to grow extremely tall, to reach sunlight above all the other branches and leaves.
Add in tall, tall trees that stretch up to the sun.

HISSSS

Give this snake some camouflage.

Plants have to compete for food on the forest floor. Scribble your own CARNIVOROUS plant that can eat passing insects.

BZZZ

MOVING PICTURES

When you 'see', your brain creates an image using information from your eyes. The image lingers briefly, so if you combine images fast enough, they overlap and appear to MOVE.

Movie footage is actually thousands of still images, played together very quickly.

MAKE A MINI MOVIE
Copy the fish template on the right, or download it from the Usborne QUICKLINKS website. Cut the 12 boxes out and put them in order. Clip or hold them at the left hand edge, and flick through to watch the sequence.

DESIGN YOUR OWN
Now use the empty squares to create your own MINI MOVIE.

Here are some ideas:

STICK MAN

HELLO

TIPS:
Use a simple character or scene, that isn't too complicated to draw.

Make the change from one box to the next quite small, so the animation looks smooth.

BALLOON

POP

These mini movies are actually a type of OPTICAL ILLUSION. For more illusions, go to pages 56-57.

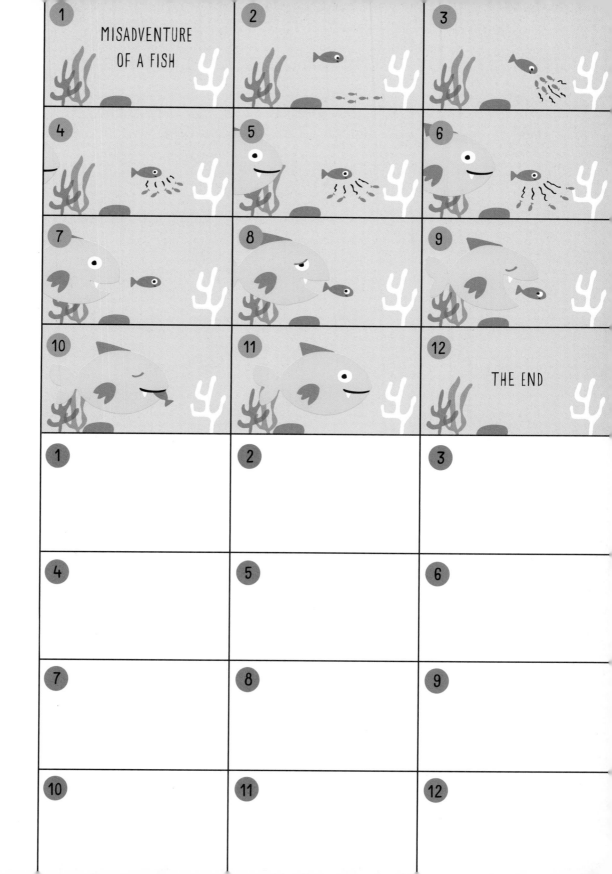

WHERE IN THE WORLD?

Cell phones can be used to track someone's location with a technique known as TRILATERATION.

Trilateration uses CELL TOWERS, which relay calls and messages to a phone. Towers can tell how far away a phone is located.

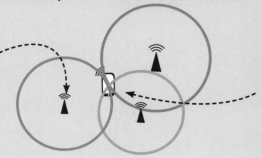

The phone is located at the point where signals from THREE TOWERS overlap.

Can you use the information from the cell towers to locate a suspect in this town? Use the clues on the right, and circle the suspect.

SUSPECT IS:

80 yards from tower A.

60 yards from tower B.

40 yards from tower C.

Circles are 20 yards apart.

The answer is on page 77.

ᴙOᴙᴙIMMIRROR WRITING

When you look in a mirror, it bounces your reflection straight back at you. This creates a MIRROR IMAGE, with everything flipped left-right.

If you raise your left hand, your reflection raises the hand facing it – which is actually the reflection's RIGHT hand.

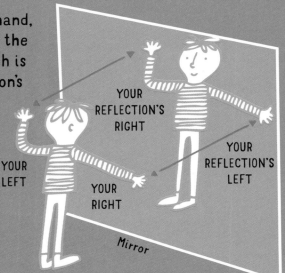

YOUR REFLECTION'S RIGHT

YOUR LEFT

YOUR RIGHT

YOUR REFLECTION'S LEFT

Mirror

Your left side becomes the right side of your reflection, and vice versa.

This is known as the RULE OF REFLECTION.

Flipped reflections are especially obvious with writing.

Ambulances and fire engines have mirror writing on their hoods, so it looks the right way around when reflected in a driver's mirror.

Italian inventor and artist Leonardo da Vinci wrote his notes backwards, in "mirror writing." Some people think it was to keep his work secret.

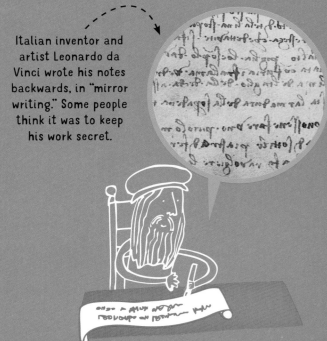

Can you decipher the message below,
to discover a famous quote of Leonardo's?

**LEARNING NEVER
EXHAUSTS THE MIND**

Try writing your own
secret message using
mirror writing.

It's easiest to use
capital letters, and
write the message the
right way around first,
then reflect it.

You could make your
message even harder
to read by taking out
the spaces, or jumbling
the words up.

FEEL THE FORCE

Forces change the way things MOVE, by pushing, pulling or dragging. You can't see forces, but they're responsible for holding the universe together, and for whenever anything in it SPEEDS UP, SLOWS DOWN or STOPS altogether.

On Earth, there are three main forces.

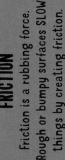

GRAVITY
PULLS things down towards the Earth.

FRICTION
Friction is a rubbing force. Rough or bumpy surfaces SLOW things down by creating friction.

AIR RESISTANCE
As things fall or travel, air PUSHES into them, SLOWING them down.

IMAGINE a ball is rolling down the ramps on this page. Follow the instructions to CHANGE how the ball moves. Write in labels or scribble pictures to show where you would put things.

To get going, add something to **SPEED UP THE BALL.**
(Tip: try reducing FRICTION.)

IDEAS FOR THINGS YOU COULD ADD IN:

Water

Oil

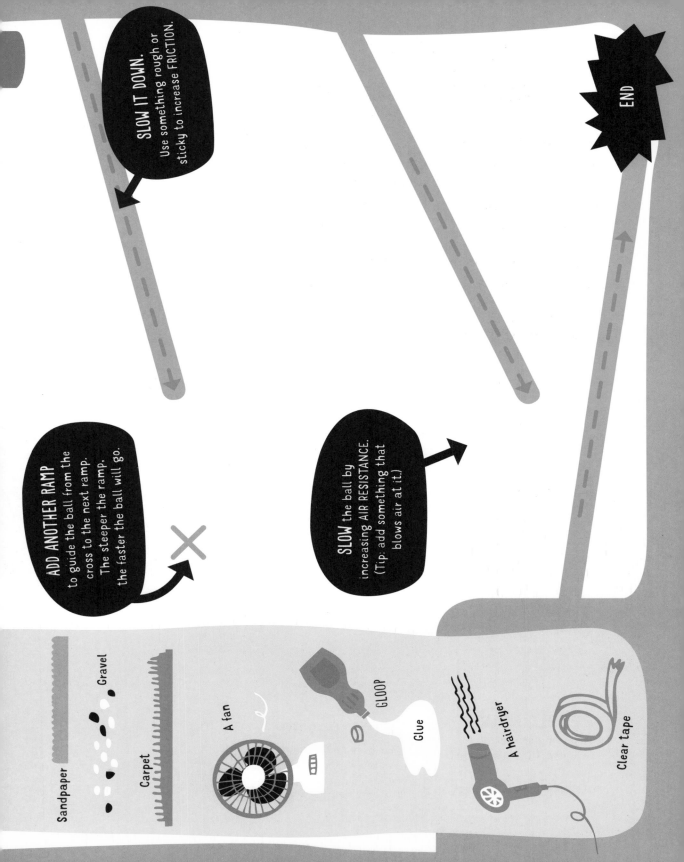

POWER TO THE PEOPLE

The electricity that powers towns and cities has to come from a POWER SOURCE. A lot of power comes from polluting sources that are fast running out, such as coal. Today, more and more is coming from RENEWABLE SOURCES – sources that can never run out.

Use the clues to work out the best spot on the map to build a power station, for each of these power sources.

Use these symbols to represent each power source.

SOLAR POWER
Sunlight is turned into electricity or used to heat water in SOLAR PANELS.

WAVE POWER
A TURBINE sits on top of the sea and generates energy as waves move.

HYDROPOWER
Flowing water turns a turbine, which is built into a DAM in a river, or a WHEEL in a waterfall.

WIND POWER
Tall TURBINES spin in the wind.

PEOPLE POWER
Stepping on specially-designed TILES generates pulses of energy, turning footsteps into usable energy.

GEOTHERMAL
Heat from under the ground in volcanic areas or hot springs can generate energy. As STEAM rises it turns a turbine.

CITY

HOT DRY DESERT

CHOPPY SEAS

GALE-FORCE COAST

VOLCANO

MOUNTAINS

WATERFALL

RIVER

TOWN

CALM BAY

The answers are on page 78.

41

TURNING TURBINES

Energy from almost all sources can be transformed into useful energy
by spinning a TURBINE connected to an electricity GENERATOR.

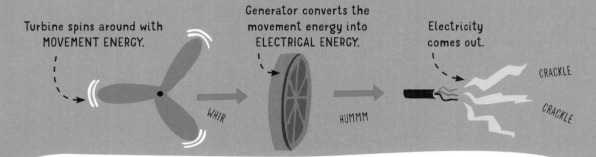

Turbine spins around with
MOVEMENT ENERGY.

WHIR

Generator converts the
movement energy into
ELECTRICAL ENERGY.

HUMMM

Electricity
comes out.

CRACKLE

CRACKLE

Almost anything that spins or turns can act as a turbine.
Use this space to think of things that turn, to which you
could attach a generator to make electricity.

WHAT ABOUT:

Merry-go-round?

Unicycle?

Wheelchair?

Through the microscope

Microscopes can magnify things many hundreds of times, revealing tiny details – including the cells which form all living things.

Match each description to the right microscopic image.

A — Magnified 10x

B — Magnified 400x

C — Magnified 1,500x

D — Magnified 80x

CELLS IN A FLOWER STEM

Cells in plant stems are PACKED TIGHTLY TOGETHER, so the stem is firm enough to stand up.

HUMAN NERVE CELLS

Nerve cells form a HUGE NETWORK inside your body. They transmit messages between the brain and the rest of the body.

BUTTERFLY WING

Butterfly wings are made of LAYERS OF SCALES. Light bouncing off different layers creates shimmering colors.

FLEAS

Fleas are TINY INSECTS. Like all insects, they have a segmented body and six legs.

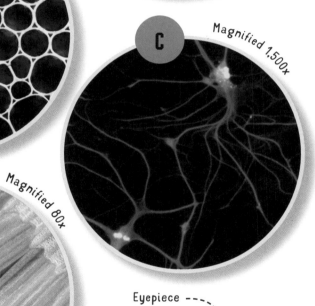

Eyepiece

Magnifying lens

Light

Focusing dial

Go to page 78 for the answers.

SEEING LIGHT

The reason you can see is because the back of your eyes are lined with cells that DETECT LIGHT. But there are no light-detecting cells where the optic nerve connects to your eye, and this creates a BLIND SPOT.

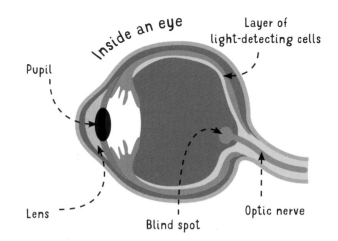

Inside an eye

Pupil

Lens

Layer of light-detecting cells

Blind spot

Optic nerve

1. To find your blind spot, SHUT ONE EYE and hold this book at arm's length – as far away as you can.

2. Focus on the triangle and VERY GRADUALLY move the book towards you.

3. At some point, the square will disappear. You've found your blind spot.

You actually have two main types of light-detecting cells in your eyes: rods and cones.

RODS help you see in LOW LIGHT and at night.

Rods are found around the EDGES of your eyes, so to see something clearly at night, such as a star, it helps not to look DIRECTLY at it.

CONES help you
to see COLORS.

Some people find it hard to tell particular colors apart, because their cones don't work well. This is known as color vision deficiency.

TEST IT: People with color vision deficiency often have trouble telling greens and reds apart. Pictures like these are used to test for color deficiency.

Can you see a number in each disc? Write down what you see.

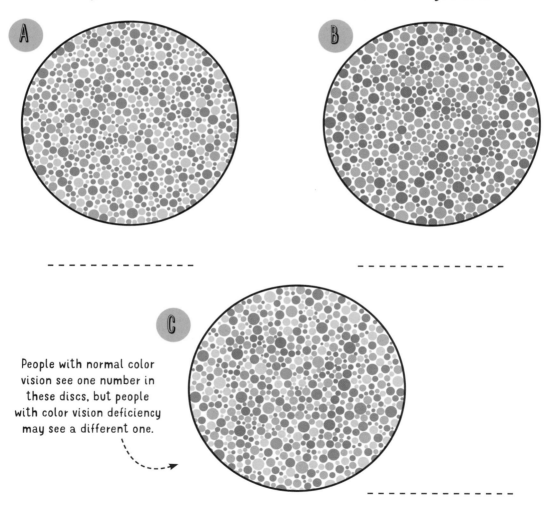

A

B

- - - - - - - - - - - - - -   - - - - - - - - - - - - - - -

C

People with normal color vision see one number in these discs, but people with color vision deficiency may see a different one.

- - - - - - - - - - - - - -

There are answers at the back of the book.

HOT AND COLD

The Sun emits waves of LIGHT that you can SEE, and HEAT that you can FEEL. The heat is known as INFRA-RED waves. Pale objects reflect infra-red waves, while dark objects absorb them.

TEST IT: Prop these pages in a patch of sunshine for at least an hour. Then feel the circles to test the effect.

RESULT: Can you feel a difference?

- -

In hot countries, many houses are painted white and people wear pale colors, to reflect heat.

Does this work with a lamp, or only with the Sun?

Most lightbulbs today are very ENERGY EFFICIENT. This means they don't waste energy as heat – so they don't make things hot.

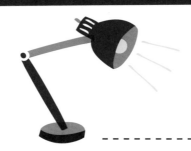

Try a variety of lamps. Did the experiment work with any of them?

- -

Solar panels are usually very dark, to absorb as much heat as possible.

Zebras live in hot places but have both white AND black stripes. Scientists think that when the black stripes absorb infra-red and the white stripes reflect it, a BREEZE is created, which cools them down.

ANIMAL JOURNEYS

Every year, many animals make huge journeys called MIGRATIONS. Imagine scientists are trying to chart the migration patterns of three species. Use the scientists' notes to work out which dots represent sightings of which species, and color them in three different colors. Then join the dots to map out where each animal has traveled.

ARCTIC

ARCTIC TERNS
These birds make the longest migration of any animal in the world. Each year they travel over 80,000km (50,000 miles).

SOUTH AMERICA

SOUTHERN HEMISPHERE

SCIENTISTS' NOTES:

Terns love the warmth - they spend summer up in the Arctic then travel south for another summer down in the Antarctic, before heading back up to the Arctic for the next summer, often in a circular route.

Terns hug the coast - they fly along the edges of continents, not right across the open ocean.

ANTARCTIC

○ Arctic tern sightings

48

WILDEBEEST

Wildebeest travel throughout the year in search of fresh grass and clean water.

Wildebeest sightings

NORTHERN HEMISPHERE

AFRICA

EQUATOR

The answers are on page 79.

SCIENTISTS' NOTES:

Wildebeest move in a circular route around the plains of Africa.

They are furthest south in the winter, when calves are born, then move north in the summer months.

HUMPBACK WHALES

Enormous humpback whales swim thousands of miles each year, between feeding sites and breeding sites.

Humpback sightings

SPLASH

SCIENTISTS' NOTES:

Humpbacks spend their time in two main locations: cold Antarctic waters for feeding, and warm tropical seas for breeding.

The whales go back and forth between these two locations over the year.

49

SKELETONS

Your skeleton is made of rigid BONES
which hold you up and protect your insides.
Joints between bones allow your body to flex and move.

MAKE A MODEL

Copy the template opposite, or download
it from the Usborne QUICKLINKS website.

Cut out the pieces and punch out
the holes. Attach matching numbers
together to make joints.

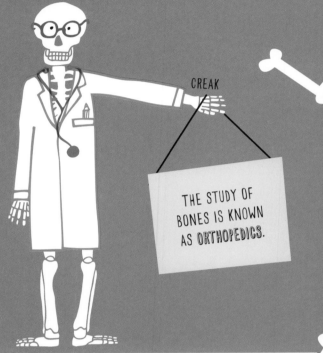

CREAK

THE STUDY OF
BONES IS KNOWN
AS ORTHOPEDICS.

WHAT TO USE:
HOLES: hole punch or sharp pencil
JOINTS: split pins or string

Your bones move because of MUSCLES,
which are attached to bones by tough
cords known as TENDONS.

TEST IT:

Lay your left hand on a table.

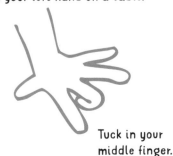

Tuck in your
middle finger.

Try lifting each finger.
Is there one you can't lift?
Circle it here.

Your third and fourth fingers
are connected to the SAME
TENDON. Tucking in your third
finger means this tendon
can't move, so you can't
lift up the fourth finger
much – if at all.

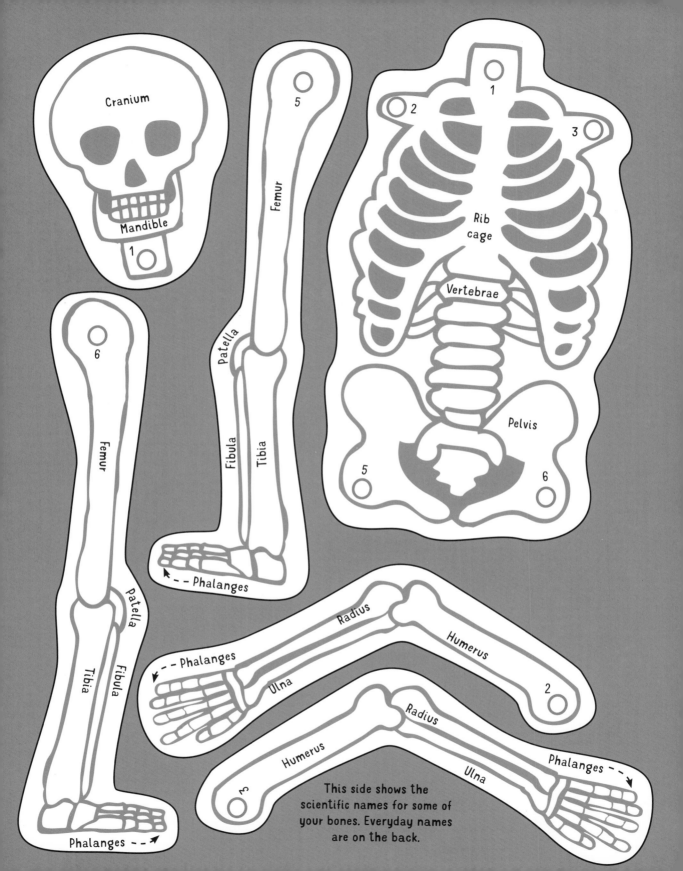

This side shows the scientific names for some of your bones. Everyday names are on the back.

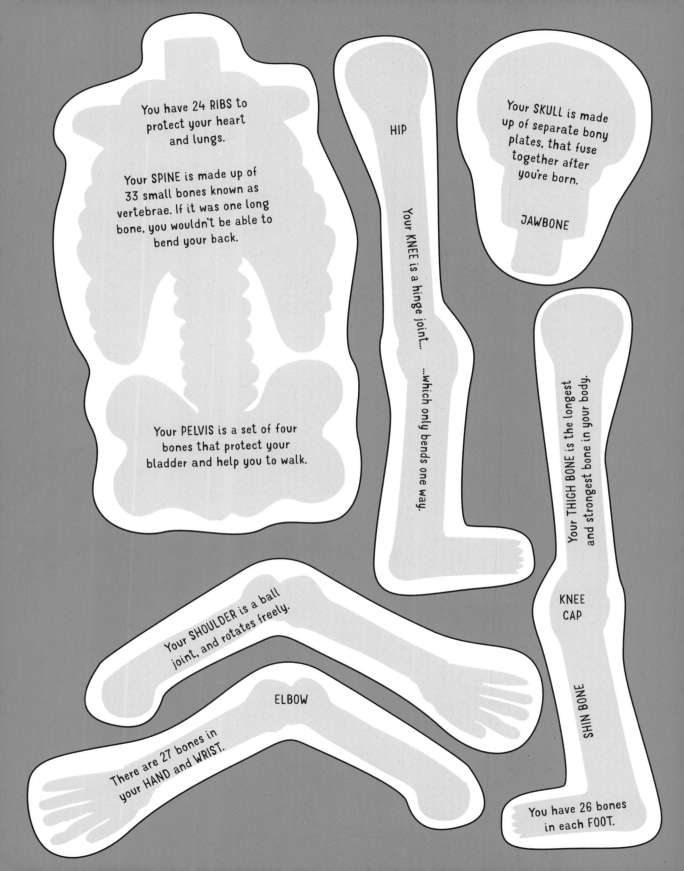

You have 24 RIBS to protect your heart and lungs.

Your SPINE is made up of 33 small bones known as vertebrae. If it was one long bone, you wouldn't be able to bend your back.

Your PELVIS is a set of four bones that protect your bladder and help you to walk.

HIP

Your KNEE is a hinge joint... ...which only bends one way.

Your SKULL is made up of separate bony plates, that fuse together after you're born.

JAWBONE

Your THIGH BONE is the longest and strongest bone in your body.

KNEE CAP

SHIN BONE

Your SHOULDER is a ball joint, and rotates freely.

ELBOW

There are 27 bones in your HAND and WRIST.

You have 26 bones in each FOOT.

BUTTERFLY OR MOTH?

LEPIDOPTERISTS, biologists who study butterflies and moths, use the features below to tell the difference between the two groups of creatures.

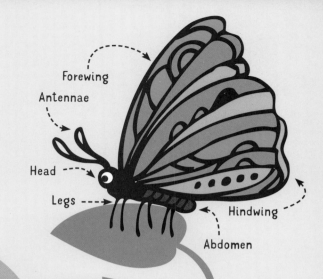

Forewing

Antennae

Head

Legs

Hindwing

Abdomen

Butterflies tend to have bold, BRIGHT PATTERNS, on the top side of their wings.

Moths tend to have DULL wings to help them BLEND IN.

Moths usually have FEATHERY antennae and HAIRY bodies.

Butterflies rest with their WINGS TOGETHER.

Butterflies have THIN antenna and SMOOTH bodies.

Moths rest with their WINGS OPEN.

Use the clues to work out which two of these are moths and which two are butterflies.

A _ _ _ _ _ _ _ _ _ _ _ _

B _ _ _ _ _ _ _ _ _ _ _ _

C _ _ _ _ _ _ _ _ _ _ _ _

D _ _ _ _ _ _ _ _ _ _ _ _

FLAP FLAP

Go to page 79 for the answers.

ROBOT DESIGNER

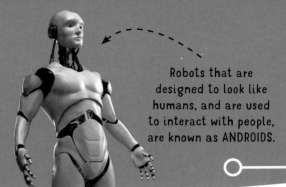

Robots are machines that are specifically programmed to do particular tasks.

Robots that are designed to look like humans, and are used to interact with people, are known as ANDROIDS.

Use this space to design your own robot.

What will it be used for?

Making sandwiches?

Taking photographs?

Walking the dog?

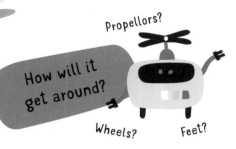

How will it get around?

Propellors?

Wheels?

Feet?

How do you want it to look?

A box with arms and legs?

An android?

A flying drone?

Lots of arms for different tasks?

What tools does it need?

A magnet to attract metal?

Claws to pick things up?

Flying robot DRONES have powerful cameras on them for photographing remote landscapes.

INDUSTRIAL robots are used in factories, and are built with the tools to do specific tasks. This one is welding car exhausts.

Some robots do jobs that are too dangerous for people. This BOMB DISPOSAL robot has a camera and a remote control unit, so it can be operated from a safe distance.

ROBOT NAME: _

TASK: _

TRICKING YOUR EYES

Your brain is constantly taking in and interpreting information from your eyes. Sometimes your brain makes mistakes, making you "see" things that aren't really there...

The FLOATING finger

Hold your hands like this.

focus on something behind your fingers.

A floating finger will appear.

The floating finger appears where information from both your eyes OVERLAPS. Your brain tries to merge the information, creating a false image.

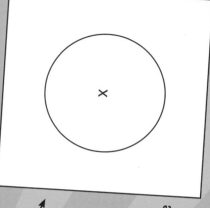

Color this circle pink, and the background green. Stare at it for 30 seconds, then look at the white box below. What happens to the colors?

AFTER images

Stare at the X for 30 seconds. Then look at the white box below. What do you see?

X

Draw a simple shape in this box, with the X in the middle. Use a bold color to fill it in.

Stare at it for 30 seconds then look up to the white box. Did your shape leave an afterimage?

The image you see when you look away is known as an AFTERIMAGE. It appears because cells in your eyes keep working even after you've stopped staring at something.

When you look at a strong color for a long time, the cells that detect that color become exhausted. When you look away, other cells take over until the original ones recharge, and you see the opposite color to the one you were looking at.

The Periodic Table

Everything in the universe is made from elements, which themselves are formed of tiny parts called atoms. Scientists organize the elements into a grid called the PERIODIC TABLE, where they're put in order, and grouped together by their PROPERTIES – how they look and behave.

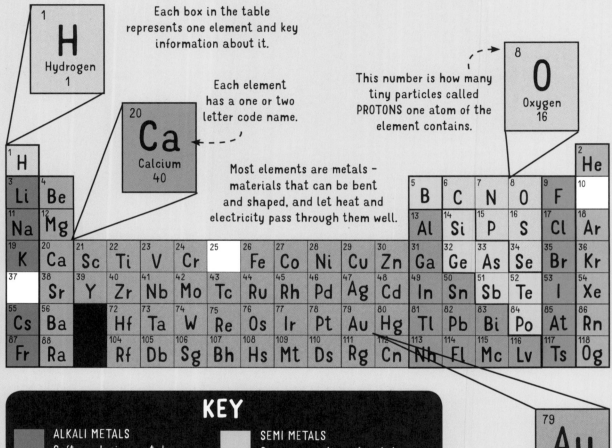

Each box in the table represents one element and key information about it.

1
H
Hydrogen
1

Each element has a one or two letter code name.

20
Ca
Calcium
40

This number is how many tiny particles called PROTONS one atom of the element contains.

8
O
Oxygen
16

Most elements are metals – materials that can be bent and shaped, and let heat and electricity pass through them well.

79
Au
Gold
197

This number is how HEAVY the element is.

The lightest element is hydrogen (H). The elements get heavier as you go across and down the table.

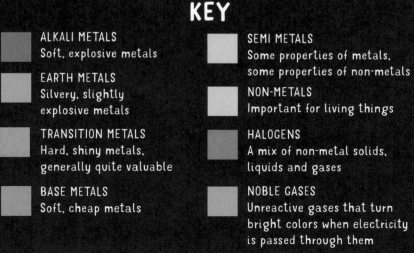

KEY

ALKALI METALS
Soft, explosive metals

EARTH METALS
Silvery, slightly explosive metals

TRANSITION METALS
Hard, shiny metals, generally quite valuable

BASE METALS
Soft, cheap metals

SEMI METALS
Some properties of metals, some properties of non-metals

NON-METALS
Important for living things

HALOGENS
A mix of non-metal solids, liquids and gases

NOBLE GASES
Unreactive gases that turn bright colors when electricity is passed through them

Work out which gap in the table these three elements slot into.
Write the code name of each element into the table
and color in the boxes to match.

Rb
Rubidium
85

PROPERTIES:

Explodes when
dropped into water

Soft metal

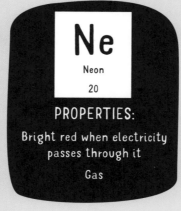

Ne
Neon
20

PROPERTIES:

Bright red when electricity
passes through it

Gas

Mn
Manganese
55

PROPERTIES:

Silvery gray
Hard metal

The answers are on page 79.

Sometimes scientists imagine a
HYPOTHETICAL element, called UNOBTAINIUM,
with ideal properties for something they want to
achieve. Invent your own unobtainium here. Think about
what it's for, and what properties it would need.

WHAT'S IT
FOR?

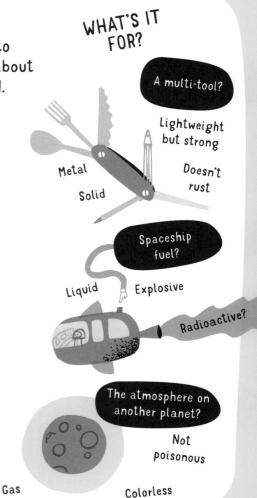

A multi-tool?

Lightweight
but strong

Metal

Doesn't
rust

Solid

Spaceship
fuel?

Liquid   Explosive

Radioactive?

The atmosphere on
another planet?

Not
poisonous

Gas   Colorless

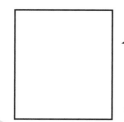

Give your element
a name, and a code
name. Write it in here.

NANOTECHNOLOGY

"Nano" means very, very small, and nanotechnology means creating and using minuscule structures roughly the size of ATOMS. A lot of nanotechnology uses CARBON atoms, which are found in all sorts of things – from substances in your body to graphite in your pencil.

In 2010, physicists Andrei Geim and Kostya Novoselov won a Nobel Prize for isolating a SINGLE LAYER of graphite.

They called this material GRAPHENE.

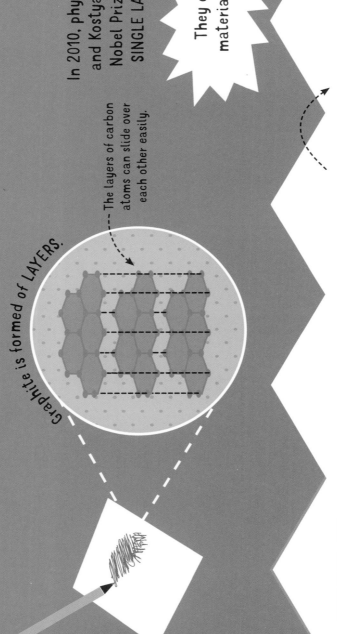

Graphite is formed of LAYERS.

The layers of carbon atoms can slide over each other easily.

1. Scribble here with a normal HB pencil – creating a patch of graphite.

TEST IT:
Try Geim and Novoselov's prize-winning method.

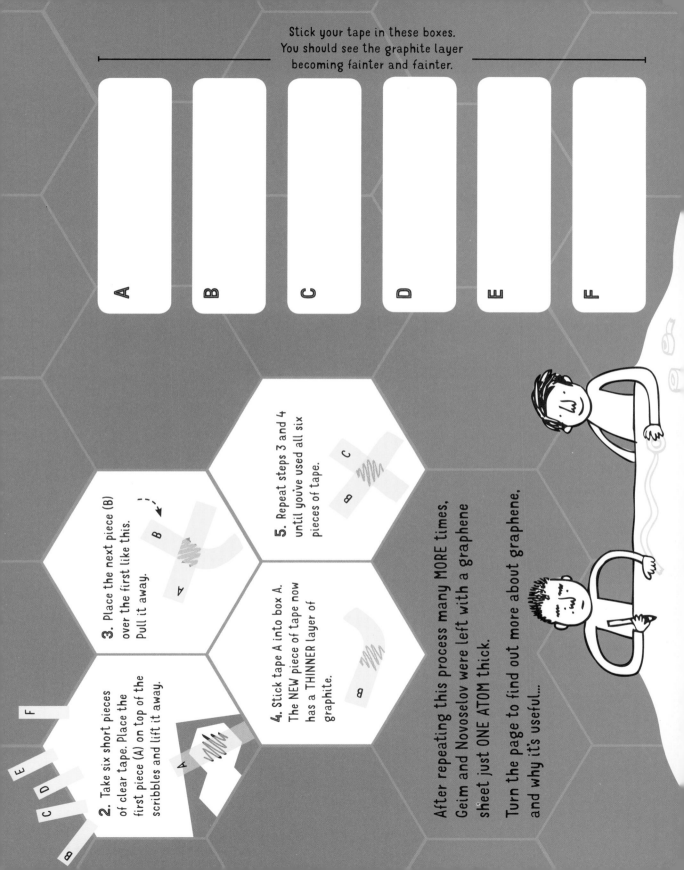

Stick your tape in these boxes. You should see the graphite layer becoming fainter and fainter.

A

B

C

D

E

F

2. Take six short pieces of clear tape. Place the first piece (A) on top of the scribbles and lift it away.

3. Place the next piece (B) over the first like this. Pull it away.

4. Stick tape A into box A. The NEW piece of tape now has a THINNER layer of graphite.

5. Repeat steps 3 and 4 until you've used all six pieces of tape.

After repeating this process many MORE times, Geim and Novoselov were left with a graphene sheet just ONE ATOM thick.

Turn the page to find out more about graphene, and why it's useful...

Graphene is the STRONGEST and most FLEXIBLE material known to science.

A sheet of graphene can be rolled up into a structure called a NANOTUBE.

Graphene sheet

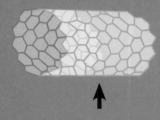

Nanotube

Nanotubes are extremely strong and light. Scientists are exploring using them to make vehicles, as well as all sorts of other things.

Use this space to design a vehicle built from nanotubes.

How will it be powered? Wheels? Wings? Sails? Rockets? Pedals?

Super-strong bike frame

Super-fast plane

ZOOOM

What's the best feature of your super-light vehicle? Extremely super-strong, super-light vehicle? Is it unbreakable? Can it be packed down fast? really small?

Light-weight sailboat

Where will it travel? Though the air? Across land? Under water? In space?

INFECTION

Viruses are tiny particles that can spread from person to person, causing INFECTIOUS DISEASES.

Imagine one person has CHICKENPOX virus. That person infects THREE others. Each of them infects THREE MORE people, then the infection DIES OUT.

Draw lines to follow the infection and work out how many people get chickenpox altogether.

Currently infected

Has never been exposed to the virus

With many viruses, once you've had it you don't get it again, and are said to be IMMUNE.

Has had chickenpox before and is immune

BEFORE VACCINATIONS

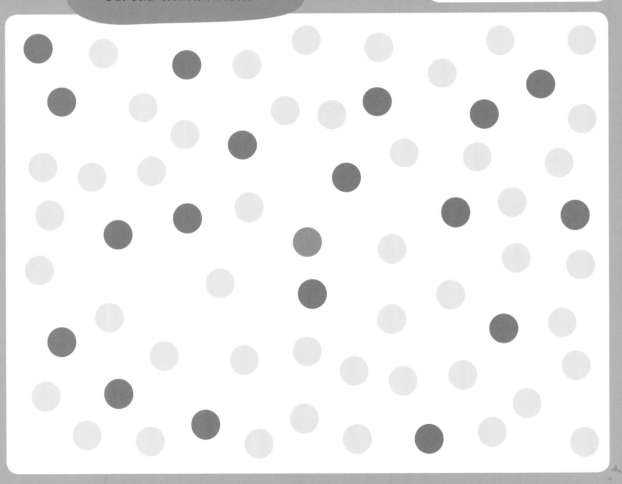

Overall, _ _ _ _ _ people got infected with chickenpox.
Once everyone has recovered, how many people are now immune? _ _ _ _ _ _ _ _

Now imagine the same people are exposed to chicken pox, except this time, some of them have had a VACCINE and become immune. Assume each person can infect THREE MORE people as before, and draw lines to follow the infection.

The chickenpox virus

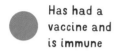
Has had a vaccine and is immune

HOW VACCINES WORK
Vaccines contain a tiny amount of a dead or weakened virus, so your body can learn how to FIGHT it, making you immune.

AFTER VACCINATIONS

This time, _ _ _ _ _ people got infected with chickenpox overall.
Now how many people are immune? _ _ _ _ _ _ _ _ _ You can find the answers on page 79.

The solar system

The solar system is the collection of PLANETS and moons that orbit our SUN.

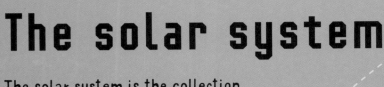

Sun

Orbit paths

Earth

It's just one small system in a great big universe, but the distances between objects in the system are still VAST.

Make your own

Copy the template on the next four pages, or download it from the Usborne QUICKLINKS website. Cut out the strips and stick them together.

Each strip has a number.

2

1

Stick the strip with the NEXT number on top, so it looks like this.

2

Make sure there's no green showing where it joins.

When all the strips are joined, you can lay it out to get a sense of the TRUE DISTANCES out in the solar system.

Each centimeter on the model represents 20 MILLION KILOMETERS in real life.

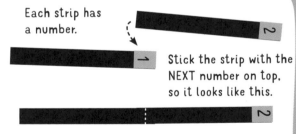

1cm
= 20,000,000km

You can see distances in miles on the reverse of the strip.

The distances from the Sun are to scale, but sizes of the planets are NOT.

(If they were, at this scale the Sun would be a dot, and the planets would be too small to see).

SUN

The Sun is the center of our solar system.

MERCURY

57 million kms away from the Sun

VENUS

108 million kms away

EARTH

150 million kms away

The Moon is the furthest humans have ever been.

MARS

228 million kms away

ASTEROID BELT   329-478 million kms away

The asteroid belt sits between Mars and Jupiter, and is about 150 million kms wide. It is full of rocky asteroids, also known as minor planets.

JUPITER

779 million kms away

Jupiter is the largest planet. It's so big the Earth could fit inside it over 1,300 times.

Saturn and Jupiter are known as gas giants, because they are made almost entirely of the gases hydrogen and helium.

SATURN

The rings around Saturn are made of ice.

1.43 billion kms away

Planets are held in orbit by the Sun's strong gravitational pull.

MARS
142 million
miles away

EARTH
93 million
miles away

SATURN
889 million
miles away

VENUS
67 million
miles away

MERCURY
36 million miles
away from the Sun

ASTEROID BELT
204-297 million miles away

SUN

JUPITER
484 million
miles away

URANUS

Uranus and Neptune are known as ice giants, because they are made of heavy, frozen methane and ammonia.

2.88 billion kms away

Most of the empty vastness of space is just that... space. There is the occasional speck of dust, and a few atoms of gas, but it's mostly lots and lots of nothing.

The dwarf planet PLUTO is another billion kilometers this way...

NEPTUNE

4.5 billion kms away

A probe called VOYAGER was launched in 1977 to explore the outer reaches of the solar system. It passed Neptune in 1989, and left the solar system altogether in 2012 – the furthest a human-made object has ever gone – and it's still going.

URANUS
1.78 billion
miles away

NEPTUNE
3.67 billion
miles away

Fingerprints

The people who investigate crime scenes, searching for fingerprints, are called FORENSIC SCIENTISTS. Each person's fingerprints are UNIQUE and unlike anyone else's, so prints are a good way to prove who was at the scene.

AHA!

What do your fingerprints look like?

TEST IT: Scribble in this circle with an ordinary HB pencil, until you have a solid patch of dark gray.

Press one of your fingers over the patch, then press it down in this empty box.

Try several fingers.

There are three main TYPES of fingerprints.
Which do you have?

Arch   Loop   Whorl

My type:

- - - - - - - - - - - - - - - - - -

Scientists aren't sure how fingerprints form, but they are affected by the conditions you experienced inside the womb. As no two people experienced *exactly* the same conditions, no two people's fingerprints are exactly the same.

Even identical twins have different fingerprints.

THOUGHT EXPERIMENTS

A lot of science is about doing experiments, but sometimes it's impossible to try things out, and you can only THINK about what MIGHT happen. This is known as a THOUGHT EXPERIMENT.

Physicist Albert Einstein posed some of the most famous thought experiments...

What do you think?

What would Earth look like if humans had never existed? Scribble your ideas and sketches here.

If you throw a ball inside a moving train, what speed does the ball move?

Would the land look different?

Would Earth be better or worse off, or neither?

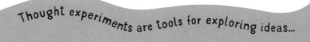

Thought experiments are tools for exploring ideas...

72

Does TIME SLOW DOWN when you travel at the speed of light?

What would I see if I was traveling at the SPEED OF LIGHT?

WHOOOOOSH

Einstein used math and facts he did know to suggest answers to his questions. Scientists today think his ideas were mostly right.

If there's life on other planets, what might it look like?

Would it look anything like life on Earth?

Are there lots of different species as on Earth - or just one?

Do the creatures have bodies, or are they single cells, like bacteria?

There are no right or wrong answers.

BREAKTHROUGH!

Look for clues to help you match the scientists to their famous DISCOVERY, THEORY or INVENTION.

Isaac Newton

Florence Nightingale

Alexander Fleming

Ada Lovelace

Marie Curie

Antoine Lavoisier

DISCOVERED:
**OXYGEN
IN 1778**
Realized that things burn in the air, and that oxygen helps them burn.

INVENTED:
**NEW TYPES OF GRAPH
IN 1856**
Also developed statistics and founded modern nursing.

INVENTED:
**FIRST COMPUTER PROGRAM
IN 1842**
Wrote it to predict a sequence of numbers called Bernoulli numbers.

DISCOVERED:
**HOW GRAVITY WORKS
IN 1687**
Was inspired when an apple fell from a tree – so the story goes...

DISCOVERED:
**RADIOACTIVITY
IN 1903**
Became the first woman to win a Nobel Prize. In fact, she won two.

DISCOVERED:
**PENICILLIN
IN 1928**
Penicillin grows as mold, and kills bacteria. It is now used as a medicine.

The answers are on page 80.

If you were to be a famous scientist,
what would you like to invent or discover?
Write, draw, design or describe your
invention or discovery here...

A computer scientist
who creates a truly
intelligent robot?

An engineer
who designs the
tallest building
in the world?

A physicist who
finally comes up
with a unifying
theory of
everything?

A biologist
who discovers
a new
species?

A chemist who
finds a brand
new element?

An astronomer
who discovers a
planet no one
has seen before?

20–21 ANIMAL IDENTIFIER

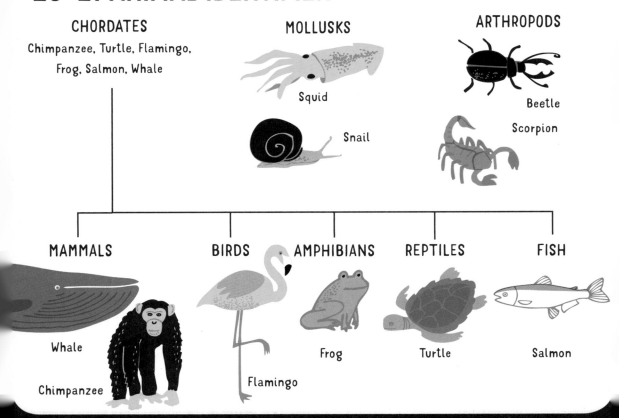

CHORDATES
Chimpanzee, Turtle, Flamingo, Frog, Salmon, Whale

MOLLUSKS
Squid
Snail

ARTHROPODS
Beetle
Scorpion

MAMMALS
Whale
Chimpanzee

BIRDS
Flamingo

AMPHIBIANS
Frog

REPTILES
Turtle

FISH
Salmon

22–25 MAKING A MOVE

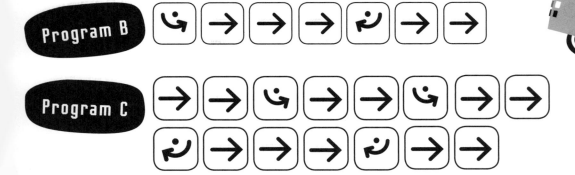

Program B ↱ → → → ↪ → →

Program C → → ↱ → → ↱ → → ↪ → → → ↪ → →

22–25 MAKING A MOVE CONT.

Program D

Broken Program

Debugged Program

 Program E =
Robot: **2**

 Program F =
Robot: **1**

---

26 LIGHT MAZE

The light illuminates F.

28–29 THE SKY AT NIGHT

THERE ARE:
3 meteors
50 stars
1 satellite
2 planets
1 Moon

Ursa Major

---

35 WHERE IN THE WORLD

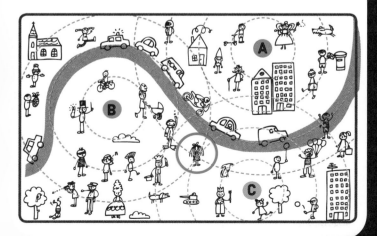

36–37 MIRROR WRITING

The secret message says
"Learning never exhausts the mind"

40–41 POWER TO THE PEOPLE

You could put a hydropower station in the river, but you can generate MORE energy at the waterfall, where water is flowing very fast.

You could put the people power tiles in the town, but as the city is bigger they will probably generate more energy there.

43 THROUGH THE MICROSCOPE

A
Fleas

B
Cells in a flower stem

C
Human nerve cells

D
Butterfly wing

45 SEEING LIGHT

DISC A - 15
DISC B - 57
DISC C - 74

People with color vision deficiency may see **21** in disc **C**.

IMPORTANT:
Don't worry if you don't see what the answers say. These discs are just reproductions, and are three examples from a much bigger collection. Color printing may vary, and this is not a substitute for a test by an optician.

48–49 MIGRATION

Arctic tern

Wildebeest

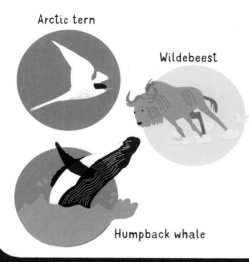

Humpback whale

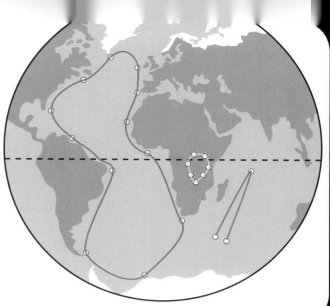

53 BUTTERFLY OR MOTH

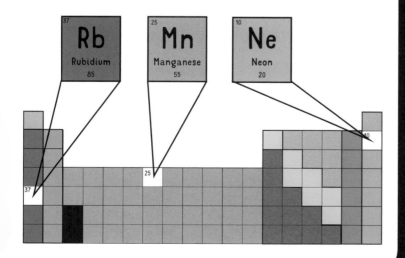

A   Butterfly   B   Butterfly   C   Moth   D   Moth

58–59 PERIODIC TABLE

37		25		10	
Rb		**Mn**		**Ne**	
Rubidium		Manganese		Neon	
85		55		20	

64–65 INFECTION

BEFORE VACCINATIONS:
Overall **13** people got infecte
Once everyone recovered
31 were immune.

AFTER VACCINATIONS:
11 people got infected.
Now all **65** people
are immune.

74 BREAKTHROUGH!

Isaac Newton
DISCOVERED:
HOW GRAVITY WORKS

Florence Nightingale
INVENTED:
NEW TYPES OF GRAPH

Alexander Fleming
DISCOVERED:
PENICILLIN

Ada Lovelace
INVENTED:
FIRST COMPUTER PROGRAM

Marie Curie
DISCOVERED:
RADIOACTIVITY

Antoine Lavoisier
DISCOVERED:
OXYGEN

Photographic credits: p.12 - Artist's concept of a NASA Mars exploration rover, Courtesy of NASA/ JPL-Caltech. p.36 - Leonardo da Vinci's writing © Science, Industry and Business Library, General Collection/New York Public Library/Science Photo Library. p.43 - Fleas, SEM © Steve Gschmeissner/ Science Photo Library; Lily stalk, SEM © Marek Mis/Science Photo Library; Brain cells, SEM © Nancy Kedersha/UCLA/Science Photo Library; Butterfly wing SEM © Frank Fox/Science Photo Library p.53 - A) Adonis blue butterfly © Heath McDonald/Science Photo Library; B) Swallowtail butterfly © Leslie J Borg/Science Photo Library; C) Rosy footman moth © Nigel Downer/Science Photo Library; D) Polyphemus moth © Matt Meadows/Science Photo Library. p.54 - Android © Science Picture Co/ Science Photo Library. p.55 - Drone © Didier Lebrun/Reporters/Science Photo Library; Welding robot © David Parker, 600 Group Fanuc/Science Photo Library; Bomb disposal robot © Spencer Grant/Science Photo Library

With many thanks to the Isshinkai Foundation, Tokyo, Japan, for their permission to reproduce the table in the Ishihara Test for Color Deficiency, on page 45.

First published in 2018 by Usborne Publishing Ltd., Usborne House, 83-85 Saffron Hill, London EC1N 8RT, England. www.usborne.com Copyright © 2018 Usborne Publishing Ltd.